# Our Family Broke

## Parental Alienation

The author of this book does not endorse any form of treatment or medical advice. The intent of this book is how adult decisions affect Alienated Parents, **Alienated Children,** and Targeting Parents.

This is a true story of the lives of 2 Adult Children of Parental Alienation. Any other character likenesses are of pure coincidence. This is one story out of millions of children attempting to survive Parental Alienation. This book offers NO advice directly or indirectly. The Publisher and Author assume NO legal responsibility or otherwise, for your behavior. It is understood that readers of this book hold harmless all that participated in bringing this book together.

It is the author's greatest wish that this book exposes a very sensitive subject that causes extreme lifelong psychological and emotional pain. Almost all children do NOT even know they are being abused!

When reading with children, it would be BEST not to identify illustrated characters with actual family members.

There are questions at the end of this book that will help you understand how and why your children feel.

Our Prayers and Love go to all those suffering.

This book is dedicated to our Alienated father:

Lloyd Elliott Paioff, RIP 1947-1993

"We are twin Otters. I'm Jussie."

"And I'm Jules. We have the same problem but feel differently about it."

Jussie stutters, "I'm so sad, I have a lump in my throat and my tummy feels yucky and I'm trying not to cry. I don't want anyone to see me cry. I just feel really tired and want to hide."

Jules screams, "I'm very angry! My face feels hot and turns red. I want to yell and smash things!"

Jussie says, "Our parents are Popper and Rory. We lived in the water for a long time in Kelp Forest, which is a lot like tall seaweed."

Jules adds, "We had lots of love, friends and played all day together."

Jussie continues, "During the day Popper and Rory would groom us often. They taught us to swim, fish, crack mussels on rocks, protect us from drowning, and kept us away from hunters on boats. Fish were always near hunter's boats. Popper was funny because mussels could be cracked on the tummy using rocks, and Popper made silly sounds that everyone liked to hear."

"At night we all held paws to make a raft and the waves couldn't

separate our family while we slept so we would stay safe. We loved our

life." Jules reminisces.

Our Raft

"As we grew up," Jules continues, "Popper and Rory started to argue.

They were loud and they wouldn't share fish with each other! We felt

scared and hid."

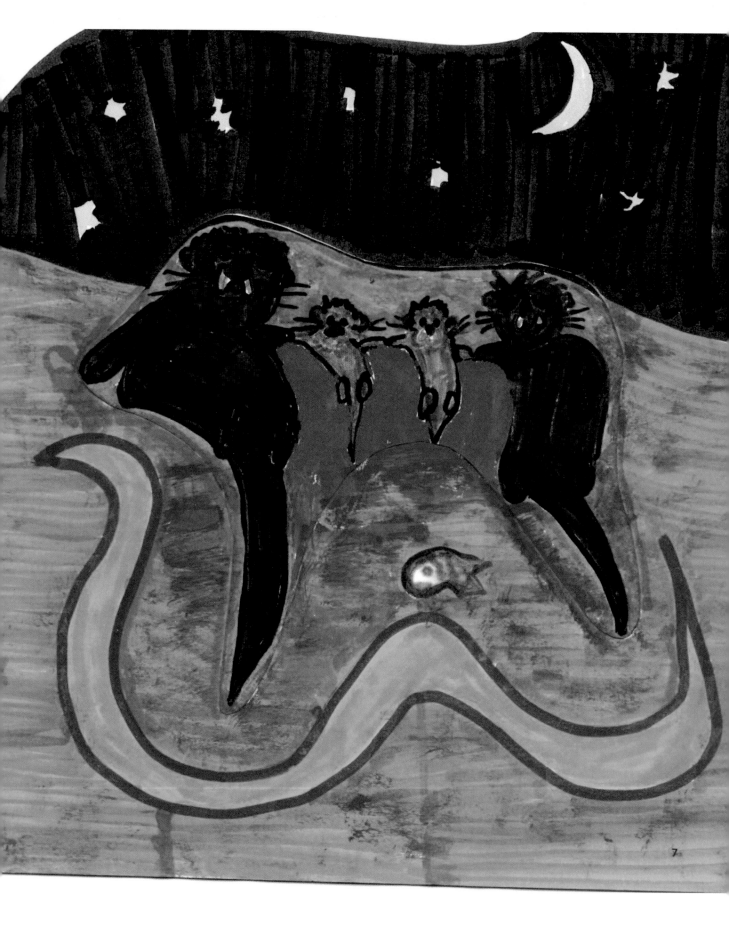

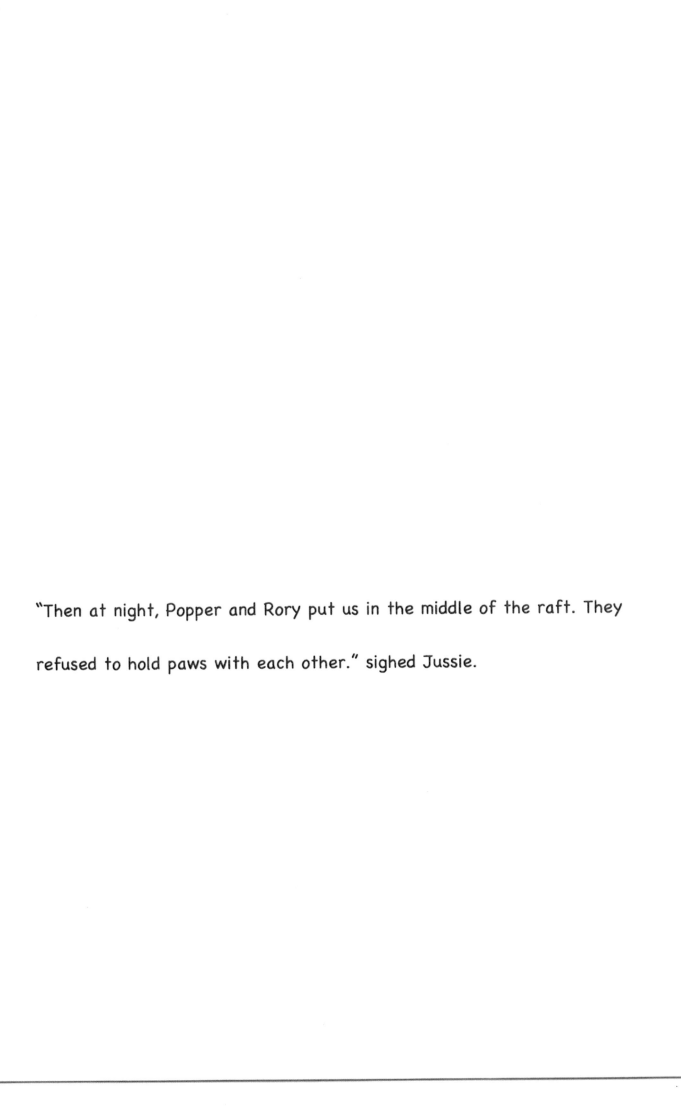

"Then at night, Popper and Rory put us in the middle of the raft. They

refused to hold paws with each other." sighed Jussie.

"Then suddenly, Rory swam very fast away from Popper, and forced us out of Kelp Forest!" explained Jules sadly.

Jussie had begged Rory, "Please can we stay at Kelp Forest? You don't need to hold Popper's paws as part of our raft. Please stay in Kelp Forest."

Rory didn't listen or care about Jussie's, Jules, or Popper's feelings.

"Rory made us swim for 4 hours to an unfamiliar place called Long Seaweed! We were very far from Kelp Forest, and we missed Popper even more. Our hearts were broken." cried Jules.

"One day Popper came to visit us! We were very happy to see Popper and Popper was very happy to see us!" Jules said excitedly.

Popper said something very important to us. "No matter, whatever happens, I will always LOVE both of you."

"But Rory was angry and got very loud. We felt scared and hid. Popper

never came back to visit us." Said Jussie sadly.

"Popper is bad and could kidnap you!" Rory shouted, "Popper would have you swim near hunter's boats, and you could be killed! Popper can't fish, so if you go to Popper, you won't have food."

Rory scared us and controlled us. "Popper loves friends and doesn't love you anymore!" Continued Rory.

Then Jules and Jussie looked at each other and said at the same time,

"But, Popper loves us."

Jussie said, "We did the same things we always did, but with a sad heart. We swam, fished, cracked mussels, held paws while sleeping. Rory had lots of friends that said leaving Popper would be best for us, but we didn't think that was true. Rory said lots of bad things about Popper and we started to believe some of it."

Jussie and Jules missed Popper so much that it hurt their hearts all the time, but they kept ACTING like everything was fine.

"But everything wasn't fine", said Jules. Jussie nodded in agreement.

They felt stuck at Long Seaweed and didn't know how to get back to Kelp Forest. Every single night, Jules and Jussie would dream about being home at Kelp Forest with Popper and Rory when everything used to be happy. They missed their friends, relatives, Kelp Forest, but most of all they missed Popper.

Jussie and Jules stopped talking about Popper because Rory would yell at them when they did. It felt like Popper was erased. Rory told them they would never see Popper again!

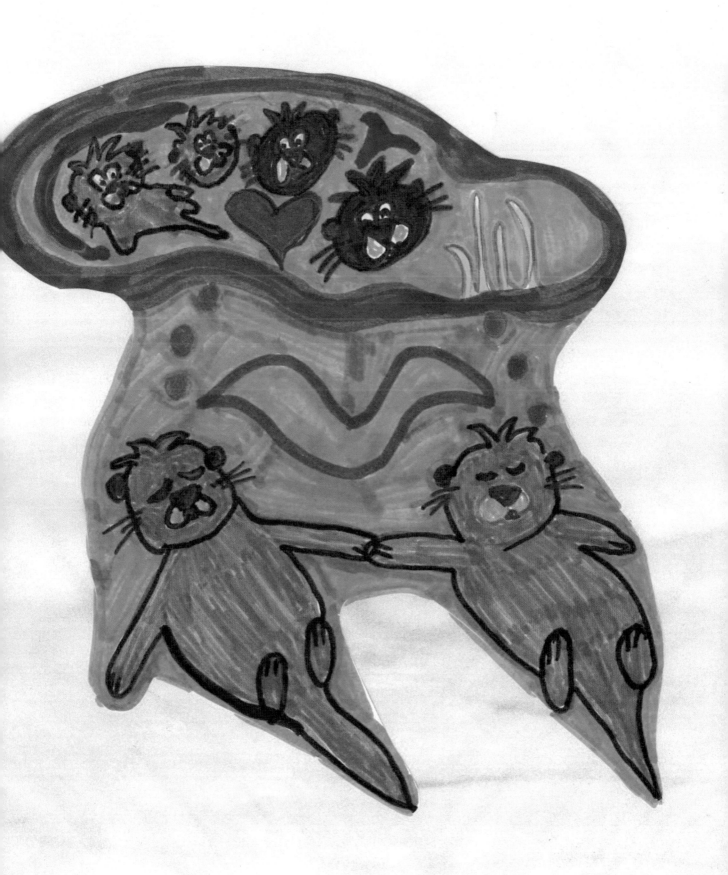

Rory began to do dangerous things with friends like swim too close to

the hunter's boats where it was much easier to catch fish.

Rory did not make good decisions.

Rory then met Barfy. Jussie begged Rory not to hold paws at night with Barfy while they slept as a raft. Jussie watched Barfy carefully and could see Barfy was not nice.

"Barfy was very mean to us!" said Jules. "Barfy hated Popper and tried to make us hate Popper even though Barfy never met Popper."

Barfy told Rory and Jules they were going to move to Rocky Land.

"Then Barfy told me that I would be left alone at Long Seaweed." exclaimed Jussie.

Barfy moved Rory and Jules to Rocky Land without me. I was left all alone, abandoned, the same way Rory had abandoned Popper." Why would Rory allow this? "Everyone else moved to Rocky Land and I would be left by myself," said Jussie, "I missed Jules and Popper.

When they got to Rocky Land, Barfy would bark loudly at Rory. Jules tried to protect Rory from Barfy, but Barfy was bigger and tried scaring Jules with BIGGER teeth and loud roar. Rory didn't like that, so for a little while Barfy was not allowed to come back to Rocky Land.

Then one day, Barfy came back. Jules didn't feel safe living with Barfy in Rocky Land and moved back to Long Seaweed near Jussie.

That's how our family Broke," cried Jules.

Time had gone by, and Jussie was older and decided to try to find the way back to Kelp Forest and swam all alone to see Popper. Popper was very old and sick. Jules came immediately. Popper still tried to make funny sounds to make us laugh, but one day Popper sank down to the bottom of the ocean never to be seen again.

Jules and Jussie were shocked! Jussie held in all the grief and began to have lots of body pain all over. Many times, Jussie had to go to the doctor because Jussie had too much trauma and stress growing up without Popper. The doctors would have to do lots and lots of surgeries because the stress hurt Jussie's heart and body so much. Jussie refused to talk about feelings, and never showed any emotions. Jussie was numb.

If Jussie had a safe grown-up otter that could be trusted, then Jussie would not have kept all the heartbreak inside. Jussie would have talked about feelings and been healthier in mind and heart.

But the grown-up otters were very busy with their own lives. They kept telling Jussie it was safer this way.

Some of Popper's longtime friends were meeting together to remember Popper, but Rory told Jussie and Jules not to go, even though they didn't live with Rory. "Rory still controlled us!" yelled Jules.

"And that is why I'm so sad," said Jussie.

Jules said, "And that's why I'm Angry!"

So much time had gone by, they missed Popper even more than ever.

## What should they do now?

Jules and Jussie had a big decision to make because now they were grown-ups. They could stay sad and angry or find a way to heal their hearts.

Jussie becam1e independent, responsible, helpful to others, but the heartbreak stayed inside.

Jules, because of anger, swam near the hunter's boats like Rory did.

The hunters threw a spear at Jules, and it missed by only a few inches!

Jules swam away very fast!

Jules and Jussie thought about Rory. They thought about Popper and all

the time that was wasted without Popper in their lives. They thought

about how Rory kept them from Popper and said bad things about

Popper to try to make them not love Popper anymore.


They could stay angry and sad, or they could talk to a special doctor,

called a therapist. Just by talking Jules and Jussie could understand

why they felt sad and angry and create their own destiny in the here

and now.

Jules decided to enjoy life in Long Seaweed and met Jet. Jules began to

bring fish to Jet and would make silly sounds like Popper did.

Jules liked to make Jet laugh.

Jules chose not to do anything dangerous like swim near the hunter's

boats. Jet was a good stable influence on Jules.

Jules liked to take the shells that were broken from mussels and create

beautiful art pieces. That helped Jules a lot with feelings. Jules loved

to be creative. Jules sometimes thought about Popper and Rory. Jules

remembered the good days together with Jussie and Popper.

Jules cried a lot, and that helped. Jules learned it is ok to cry.

Jussie decided to hold paws and make a new raft with Geter. Geter was very nice and always wanted to help anyone at any time. Geter was older than Jussie, and Jussie felt very safe like the old days in Kelp Forest.

Jussie didn't want Rory to visit. Jussie didn't like how Rory had kept them away from Popper, and all the bad things that were said about Popper. Jussie didn't like Rory's bad decisions and how they affected Jules and Jussie. Jussie was angry because even if Jussie warned Rory that a decision was bad, Rory would do it anyway. Why did Jussie know the consequences of the bad decisions Rory made?

Jussie knew because Jussie used the brain and heart inside Jussie's body to understand how Rory's decisions would affect all of them.

Sometimes Jussie and Jules would talk about how they wanted to be away from Rory. They didn't like the dangerous, bad decisions Rory made, and how it broke their hearts when Popper was erased from their lives.

At times, Jussie was so mad thinking about losing Popper forever that Jussie would swim fast and make loud squealing noises.

For the first time, Jussie began to cry. It was time to cry. It was important to cry, even though it hurt to feel the anger and grief. It helped Jussie's heart to cry.

Jussie thought about Geter and the life Jussie chose. Even with all the surgeries from the vet, Jussie knew that now life could be what Jussie and Jules chose to make it.

Rory no longer controlled or would make decisions for Jules and Jussie EVER again.

Jules and Jussie never swam near the hunter's boats ever again. Jules and Jussie thought if they ever had baby otters, and if as grown-ups Jussie or Jules separated from the raft, the children should ALWAYS see both parents.

Sometimes Jussie would swim by their family home at Kelp Forest, but it made Jussie happy and sad at the same time thinking about how good it felt to be a real family. But the family was broken forever. Jussie never stopped missing Popper and cried a lot. Jussie still needed many surgeries. The doctor explained that when you carry hurt in your heart, it comes out in pain all over the body.

Jussie would visit Jules at Long Seaweed.

Jules and Jussie made up their own mind about how they felt about Rory. Rory had put them in a lot of danger by being with Barfy and Rory continued to swim near the hunter's boats.

Jussie and Jules talked to each other and how they would NEVER treat anyone like Barfy did. They also decided it was very important to make good decisions that were not dangerous like Rory's decisions.

Jules had also swum by Kelp Forest, but time had gone by, and life had

changed so much that Kelp Forest never looked or felt the same again.


Both Jules and Jussie created their own life. They had raised

themselves and became responsible, loving, independent, fully grown

otters.

# What Do You Think?

Do you feel loved?

Do you feel sad and cry, or try not to cry?

Do you feel angry and put yourself in danger?

Do you see both of your parents?

Does your heart hurt?

Can you find a safe grown-up to talk to?

Do you need to go to the doctor because your body hurts?

Is there anyone very mean like Barfy in your life?

Would you trust Rory?

What would you do differently if you were Jussie or Jules?

How do you think Popper felt all the years Jules and Jussie were far away?

Can you think of anything Jules and Jussie could have done to see Popper when they were too young to swim 4 hours?

How can this story help you?

If you prefer to draw instead of talk, please use this page.

Parental Alienation is not new. With over half of marriages ending in divorce, one study concluded more than 13 million children in the USA are being raised by one parent and may be victims of Parental Alienation.

A <u>healthy</u> parent knows that children need to see the other parent often.

As reported from the Irish Times, "You don't get a second chance at childhood, "adds Jack, who doesn't want to stand by and see that happen to other children. *"It's emotional abuse at the highest level."* Journalist Sheila Wayman.

Problems between parents need to be separated from children visiting the other parent frequently. The children did not create the parent's problems, but through Parental Alienation, they are subjected to Psychological Abuse that will affect them for the rest of their lives. Parental Alienation can also include brainwashing children to believe the other parent is bad and dangerous. This form of child abuse has also extended to grandparents, aunts, uncles, cousins, and others.

There are several groups in the United States right now trying to create justice for children through the legal system.

The author of this book truly lived this story and sincerely hopes that this book can help parents, and other safe grown-ups to take children's feelings into consideration. Take the time to understand your children. Use the questions on the last page to open a dialog with your child. Ask the children every day how they feel. Find out why they feel the way they do.

Please note that special care was taken by the deletion of pronouns so children from any form of family can relate to the characters. For more information, please discover what Parental Alienation Syndrome is by researching and finding support groups nearby or online. One Example: Https://pasg.info/

# Remember: Children's Feelings ARE VERY Important!

Made in the USA
Las Vegas, NV
24 November 2024

12526390R00033